Y0-AHR-696

The historical notes and receipts in italics in this book have mainly come from original sources. In addition, the authors have utilized the research papers done by the Junior League of Montclair and the practical training in open hearth cookery at the Seminars on American Culture, Cooperstown, New York.

Fanny Pierson Crane

HER RECEIPTS
1796

Confections, Savouries and Drams

★ ★ ★ ★ ★

Being a Collection of Sixty Favourites
and Including
A PROPER COLLATION AND SUPPER MENU

★ ★ ★ ★ ★ ★ ★ ★ ★

A GUIDE TO OPEN HEARTH AND BEE HIVE OVEN COOKERY

*Prepared in the 18th Century Manner
and
Adapted for Twentieth Century Use*

★ ★ ★ ★ ★

Compiled and Illustrated by
AMY HATRAK
FRANCES MILLS
ELIZABETH SHULL
SALLY WILLIAMS

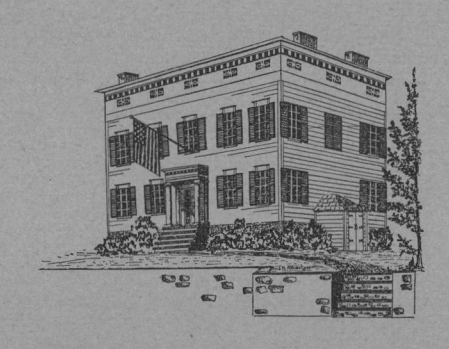

THE ISRAEL CRANE HOUSE

Built 1796
Owned and Maintained by
MONTCLAIR HISTORICAL SOCIETY, INC.
110 Orange Road
Montclair, New Jersey

COVER — A reproduction of the indigo homespun window hangings used in the Israel Crane House kitchen.
ILLUSTRATIONS OF UTENSILS — Drawn from actual early implements used in the kitchen today.

© Copyright MCMLXXIV, Montclair Historical Society, Inc.

Introduction

Welcome to the Crane House Kitchen! The little cakes are in the beehive oven, the hen is roasting in the tin kitchen, the coriander ginger cake hangs from the crane in the dutch oven, and the orange cakes hot from their iron pans are on the board waiting to be glazed with the salamander.

Is it hard to wonder then why the Crane children—Elizabeth, Abigail, Matthias, Mary and James found their way to the warm hearthside so often? Soon the visitors to the kitchen identify with Mrs. Crane and the children, by testing the beehive oven, lacing the hen until it's "done to a turn," stamping the little cakes with a hospitality print, and watching the glaze sizzle under the heat of the salamander.

The orange cake is cut, and placed on the large pewter charger, surrounded by coriander ginger slices and stamped spice crinkles. Everyone enjoys a taste. Perhaps this is the day Cranetown Mulled Cyder is poured from the noggin, or Mock Clary ladled into little cups from its iron pan warming on the hearth.

One is taken back to 1796, when Israel Crane built his imposing house on 86 acres at the foot of First Mountain, and married Fanny Pierson, daughter of a prominent Doddtown physician. Their acres were bountiful, and in the fall of the year, the time for harvesting and hog slaughtering, all the gardenstuffs and meats which were not smoked, preserved, pickled or stored in the root cellar, were hung from the kitchen rafters to dry. Today in the Crane House kitchen, we relive that era, and only foodstuffs available to the Crane family, and indigenous to New Jersey or imported for the country store at that time are utilized for the preparation of all receipts.

Israel Crane became Cranetown's most prominent citizen, and as mistress of her large home from 1796 to 1826, Fanny Pierson Crane was well known as an accomplished cook and hostess. These receipts are chosen to typify the cherished foods she prepared for her husband, family and friends. They have been prepared in the 18th century manner in the Crane House kitchen and have been adapted for 20th century use in our modern kitchens of today.

It is an honor to present them to you for your pleasure and edification.

Photo:
C. J. Owe

Contents

MEAT, FISH, AND FOWL ... PUDDINGS
Native Roasted Turkey with
    Sausage and Sage Dressing 9
Baked Elizabethtown Crab 10
Chicken Pudding 10
Baked Ham from the Smokehouse 11
Beefe Steake Pudding 12

ROOTS AND VEGETABLES
Carrot Pudding 13
Squash Pudding 14
Maced Green Beans 14
Glazed Minted Carrots 15
Mess of Pease 15

BREADSTUFFS
Crane House Pumpkin Bread 16
Beehive Oven Apricot Bread 16
Spider Corn Bread 17
Sally Lunn 17

LITTLE CAKES
Abigail's Soft Molasses Cakes 18
Benne Seed Wafers 18
Cobblestones 19
Apple Brandy Drops 19
Hospitality Thins 20
Printed Spice Crinkles 21
Rosewater Currant Cakes 21
Maids of Honor 22
Black Walnut Cakes with Maple Frosting ... 22
Rolled Holiday Cakes 23
Sunday Night Wafers 24
Miss Mary's Meringues 24

UNCOMMON CAKES AND PIES
Glazed Orange Cake 25
Coriander Ginger Cake 28

SUPPER SERVED IN THE WARMING KITCHEN 26

A PROPER COLLATION MENU 27

Contents

UNCOMMON CAKES AND PIES (Cont.)
Dutch Oven Gingerbread 28
Tansy Pie 29
Grandmother Pierson's Dated Pound Cake 30
Whiskey Apple Pie 31
Carrot Tea Cake 31

JELLIES AND PRESERVES
Madeira Wine Jelly 32
Rose Geranium Jelly 33
Crabapple Rosemary Jelly 33
Tomato-Ginger Preserves 34
Cranberry Conserve 34
Flowers and Fruit in White Wine Jelly 35

CONFECTIONS
Candied Peel 36
Whiskey Nut Balls 37
Chocolate Truffles 37
Tipsy Squire 38

Crock-Preserved Fruits 41
Greengage Plum Ice Cream 41
Rose Geranium Cream for Berries 42
Raspberry or Gooseberry Fool 42

SAVOURIES
Mushroom Savories 43
Cheddar Biscuits 44
Almonds for a Collation 44
Jersey Skillet Apples 45

DRAMS
Cranetown Mulled Cyder 46
New Jersey Stone Fence Punch 46
Rose Geranium Spiced Tea Punch 47
Mock Clary 48
Empire Room Punch 49
Rum Tea Punch 49

POTPOURRI 50

Meat, Fish and Fowl

NATIVE ROASTED TURKEY WITH SAUSAGE AND SAGE DRESSING

In our New Jersey fields and woods were grouse, quail, passenger pigeons, woodcock and the wonderful bronzed American native, the wild turkey . . . sometimes weighing as much as fifty pounds.

To dress a 14 pound turkey:
1½ large loaves of stale country or French bread
1 teaspoon salt
1 teaspoon pepper
3 tablespoons fresh thyme or 3 teaspoons dry
6 large sprigs chopped parsley
2 large onions, finely chopped
3 stalks celery, cut fine
18 ripe stoned olives, cut small
8 sprigs fresh sage, chopped, or 3 teaspoons dry
1¾ pounds fresh country sausage

Soak bread in enough milk to moisten it. Sauté onions and celery together in butter until soft but not brown. Pour into large mixing bowl. In the same skillet slightly brown the sausage, then break it into pieces with a fork. Add all remaining ingredients and stuff turkey. Sew and truss it well.

Place in a large roasting pan and cover with several layers of cheesecloth soaked in butter. Bake in a moderate (325°) oven for 5 to 5¼ hours, or until leg joint can be moved up and down with ease. Baste frequently during roasting period with butter, natural juices, and applejack right through the cheesecloth. Remove cloth during last half hour to allow bird to brown.

Garnish with fresh sage and small polished crab apples.

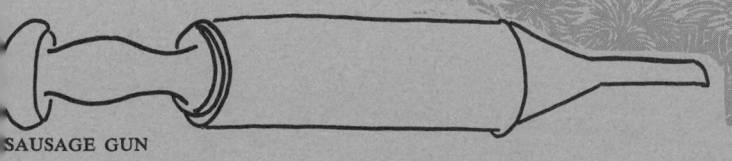

SAUSAGE GUN

BAKED ELIZABETHTOWN CRAB

Though not as plentiful as the oyster, crab was nevertheless found in local waters throughout the middle colonies.

1 pound white crab meat
4 tablespoons butter
4 tablespoons flour
½ pint cream
4 tablespoons sherry
¾ cup sharp grated cheese
½ tablespoon nutmeg, grated
½ tablespoon mace
Salt and pepper to taste
Parsley for garnishing

Flake the crab well. Make a cream sauce with the butter, flour, and cream. Add salt, pepper, and sherry. Remove from fire and add crab meat and nutmeg. Pour the mixture into a buttered iron pan. Sprinkle with grated cheddar cheese and powdered mace. Bake in moderate oven until cheese melts. Do not overcook.

When ready to serve, quickly brown with a red hot salamander or run under the broiler.

CHICKEN PUDDING

4-5 pound chicken
1 sliced celery stalk
1 halved onion
Few sprigs parsley
Pinch salt and pepper
2 teaspoons thyme
½ cup flour
1 teaspoon salt
½ teaspoon pepper
1 large onion, chopped
1/3 cup butter

Cut neck, backbone, and wings from cleaned chicken, cutting remainder into small serving pieces. Place neck, backbone, and wings in large pot; add water to cover, celery, onion half, parsley, thyme, and pinch of salt and pepper. Simmer until tender, about ¾ hour; reserve.

Combine in paper bag flour, measured salt and pepper. Shake chicken pieces in bag. Heat butter in skillet and sauté large chopped onion until golden. Add chicken pieces and sauté, turning until golden brown. Remove chicken pieces. Thicken drippings with remaining flour in paper bag, using 2 cups or more of the chicken stock.

Place chicken pieces back in pot with reserved strained stock and enough water to half cover it, lid it and simmer until tender, about 1 hour. Add thickened gravy from skillet to the pot, bubbling an additional 20 minutes. Add ½ cup cream if desired, and adjust seasoning to taste. Dust with a sprinkling of fresh or dried thyme before serving.

BAKED HAM FROM THE SMOKEHOUSE

With a ham in the smokehouse and a good frock in the press, a lady can face any occasion.

Take one Virginia or smoked ham. Soak ham overnight in cold water. Wash and remove all mold. Place ham in a large container with lid and fill ¾ full with water. (A turkey roaster will do.) Bring to a boil. Boil hard for ½ hour; reduce heat and cook slowly for about 4-5 hours, turning after 2 hours.

Remove outer skin from ham, leaving layer of fat. Coat with a mixture of brown sugar, sweet cider, and cider vinegar. Sprinkle with fresh bread crumbs. Score and dot with cloves. Brown in oven for 20 minutes.

Serve on a Leeds platter. For greater elegance, place on a ham rack and garnish with glaceed fruits or preserved seckle pears.

To Make a Country Ham

To each ham put one ounce saltpeter, one pint bay salt, one pint molasses, shake together 6 or 8 weeks, or when a large quantity is together baste them with the liquor every day; when taken out to dry, smoke three weeks with cobs or malt fumes.

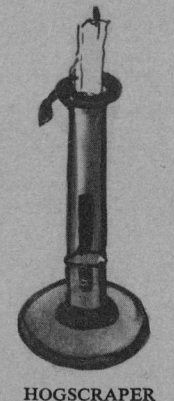

HOGSCRAPER

BEEFE STEAKE PUDDING

1 medium onion, chopped fine
1 pound top round steak in ½ inch pieces
¾ cup beef broth
¼ cup tomato juice
½ teaspoon Worcestershire Sauce
Salt and pepper
1 tablespoon butter
1 tablespoon flour
A few pieces of fresh tomato, peeled and seeded
Beef drippings or butter for browning
Yorkshire pudding batter

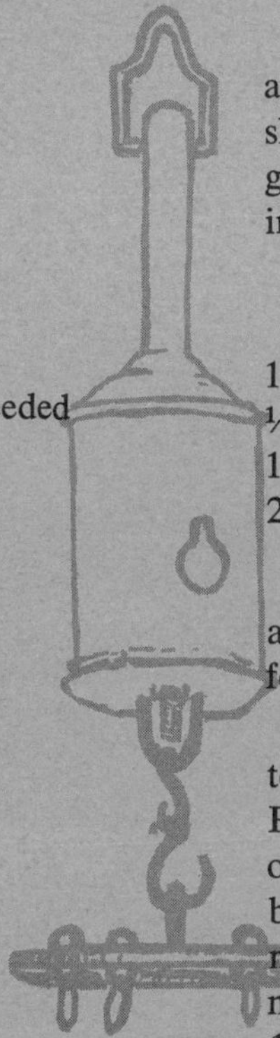

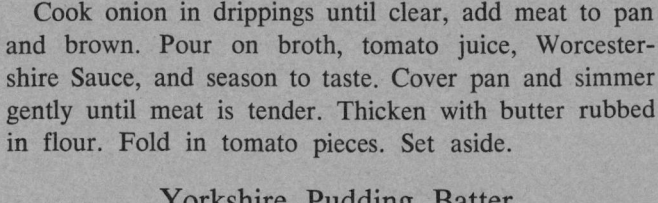

Cook onion in drippings until clear, add meat to pan and brown. Pour on broth, tomato juice, Worcestershire Sauce, and season to taste. Cover pan and simmer gently until meat is tender. Thicken with butter rubbed in flour. Fold in tomato pieces. Set aside.

Yorkshire Pudding Batter

1 cup flour
½ teaspoon salt
1 cup milk
2 eggs

Sift flour with salt into bowl. Make a well in center, add milk to well, then add eggs to milk. Beat vigorously for several minutes until batter is smooth and bubbly.

Cover bottom of 1½ quart casserole with melted butter or beef drippings. Put in a hot place until sizzling. Pour ½ quantity of Yorkshire Pudding batter into dish, or about ½ inch deep. Place in hot 450° oven and bake until puffed and set, about 15 minutes. Spread meat and gravy mixture on pudding and cover with remaining half of batter. Continue to cook in hot oven for 10-15 minutes. The outside should be crisp and golden, the inside soft.

CLOCKJACK

Roots and Vegetables

CARROT PUDDING

3 cups or 2 pounds mashed carrots
3 tablespoons butter
4 tablespoons sugar
1 cup milk
1½ tablespoons cornstarch
1 teaspoon salt
1 cup fine bread crumbs
1 cup light cream
¾ teaspoon fresh grated nutmeg
¼ cup cream sherry
3 eggs, separated

Beat egg yolks and sugar until light. Mix cornstarch with small amount of milk until dissolved. Heat remaining milk, add cornstarch and stir until smooth and slightly thickened. Blend small amount of hot thickened mixture into egg yolks and sugar. Mix well and return to remaining hot milk and cornstarch mixture, cooking over medium heat, and stirring until smooth and thick.

Add carrots, bread crumbs, butter, salt, and blend evenly. Stir in cream, add sherry and nutmeg. Mix well. Beat egg whites until firmly peaked and fold into carrot mixture.

Pour into greased 2 quart pudding pan. Place pudding pan in hot water and bake at 300° for 30 minutes; then increase to 350° and bake an additional 50 minutes.

SQUASH PUDDING

2 pounds winter squash
½ pound cheddar cheese
2 eggs
¾ cup milk
½ cup chopped onion
1 tablespoon butter
1 teaspoon grated nutmeg
Salt and pepper

TREENWARE SALT

Pare squash, remove seeds, and cut into small pieces. Boil until tender, drain well, and put into a deep baking dish. Add cheese cut into small pieces; saving a little to sprinkle on top. Saute the onion in butter. Mix into squash and cheese, and sprinkle with salt and pepper. Beat eggs to blend, add milk, then pour over the squash. Sprinkle remaining cheese on top. Dot with fresh bread crumbs and butter. Grate nutmeg on top. Bake slowly for 30 minutes or until top is delicately browned and set. Serve at once.

A salt was placed in the center of the Board. Persons of honor were seated above the salt, others below the salt; thus the expression "Worth your salt."

MACED GREEN BEANS

4 to 6 cups green beans
4 tablespoons sweet butter
Salt and pepper
1½ teaspoons mace

Swish just-picked beans in cold water and snip off ends. To make them uniform slice larger ones lengthwise down the flat side. Drop beans by the handful into 3 quarts rapidly boiling, lightly salted water. Bring water back to a boil before adding another handful of beans. Boil rapidly 6 to 8 minutes, uncovered. Test for tenderness, drain, and return to the kettle.

Add the sweet butter and lightly salt and pepper. Sprinkle generously with mace and take to the warming kitchen table.

GLAZED MINTED CARROTS

1½ pounds carrots (5 cups)
1½ cups water
1½ tablespoons butter
½ teaspoon salt
1 cup heavy cream
2 tablespoons softened butter
Freshly ground black pepper
2 tablespoons fresh peppermint
2 tablespoons sugar

If baby carrots are used, cut off tops and tips, wash, brush clean, and cook whole. Fresh young carrots should be scraped and halved. Stored winter carrots should be peeled and quartered.

Lay carrots on the bottom of a wide pan that can be covered tightly. Add water, butter, salt, and bring to a boil. Cover, and cook slowly until liquid has evaporated and carrots are almost tender, about 20 minutes. Bring cream to a boil in a small pan, and pour over the carrots. Simmer slowly, uncovered, until cream has been almost absorbed by the carrots or until the carrots are tender.

Add the softened butter, and sprinkle with sugar. Simmer a few minutes longer. Snip the fresh peppermint over the glazed carrots, and take to the table in a pewter basin.

MESS OF PEASE

To have them in perfection, they must be quite young, gathered early in the morning, kept in a cool place, not shelled until they are to be dressed; put salt in the water and when it boils, put in the pease; boil them quick according to their age; just before they are taken up add a little mint, chopped very fine; drain all the water from the pease, put in a bit of butter and serve them up quite hot.

Breadstuffs

CRANE HOUSE PUMPKIN BREAD

Pumpkins or pompions, as they were called, were grown between corn stalks utilizing space and balancing the soil. Indians taught the settlers how to dry and string them for winter use. This is a prized receipt frequently requested by Crane House guests.

1 cup corn oil
4 beaten eggs
2/3 cup water
2 cups canned pumpkin
3-1/3 cups sifted flour
1½ teaspoons salt
1 teaspoon nutmeg
1 teaspoon cinnamon
2 teaspoons baking soda
3 cups sugar
½ cup golden raisins
½ cup chopped nuts

IRON BREADPAN

Grease and flour two long loaf pans or three standard loaf pans. Mix following wet ingredients: corn oil, eggs, water, and pumpkin. Add the following dry ingredients: flour, salt, nutmeg, cinnamon, baking soda, and sugar. To combined mixture, add raisins and nuts. Bake one hour at 350°. Will stay moist for days.

BEEHIVE OVEN APRICOT BREAD

2 cups dried apricots
1 cup boiling water
4 tablespoons butter
1½ cups sugar
2 eggs, lightly beaten
3 cups flour
2 teaspoons baking soda
½ teaspoon salt
1 cup pecans, chopped

Cut dried apricots into pieces with scissors, cover with boiling water, and let stand for one hour. Cream butter and sugar, then add eggs and apricots with water in which they were soaked. Sift together flour, soda, salt, and blend dry ingredients into batter. Add nut meats. Pour into buttered bread pans, 1 large or two small. Bake in slow oven (325°) for 1 hour or until tests done.

SPIDER CORNBREAD

A long handled iron skillet with three short legs, or "spider" was placed on the hearth right over hot coals to bake this corn cake. As the coals cooled, they were removed with a long handled iron "peel," and fresh glowing coals were replaced. In this way, Mrs. Crane could maintain an even cooking temperature for slow cooking without burning the bottom of the cake.

1½ cups white corn meal, preferably water ground
1 tablespoon sugar
1 teaspoon salt
1 teaspoon baking soda
2 eggs, well beaten
2 cups buttermilk
1½ tablespoons melted butter

SPIDER

If not cooking on the hearth, preheat oven to 450°. Put an iron skillet in the oven to warm. Sift together corn meal, sugar, salt, baking soda. Add buttermilk to beaten eggs, then stir into corn meal mixture until smooth. Add melted butter.

Pour into warm skillet that has been well greased. Bake at 450° for 30 minutes.

SALLY LUNN

Hawked on the streets of London as Soleil-Lune . . . the sun and the moon . . . now a lovely yeast bread baked in a Turk's head mold—and known as Sally Lunn.

2 packages dry yeast
2 teaspoons salt
1/3 cup sugar
3 eggs
4 cups flour sifted
¼ cup water
½ cup shortening
1 cup milk

Heat the milk, water, and shortening until very warm —about 120°. Blend one-third of the flour, sugar, salt, and dry yeast in a large mixing bowl. Blend warmed liquids into flour mixture, beating with an electric mixer at medium speed for 2 minutes. Gradually add another third of the remaining flour, then the eggs, and beat at high speed for 2 minutes. Add the remaining flour and mix well. Cover and let rise in a warm place until double in bulk, then beat down well with a wooden spoon.

Pour into a well greased iron or earthen Turk's head mold, and let rise again until almost double in bulk. Bake in a moderate oven (350°) for approximately 40 minutes.

Turn out on a pressed glass cake stand and serve at tea time with rose geranium jelly. Unsurpassed when served piping hot with butter and marmalade.

Little Cakes

ABIGAIL'S SOFT MOLASSES CAKES

These little cakes are a favourite with Crane House visitors of all ages. They should be soft and large. Serve hot with cool milk from the Springhouse.

2½ cups sifted flour
2 teaspoons baking soda
1 teaspoon ginger
1 teaspoon cinnamon
¼ teaspoon salt
½ cup soft butter or margarine
½ cup sugar
½ cup molasses
1 egg
¼ cup cold water
1 cup light raisins

Sift flour, baking soda, ginger, cinnamon, and salt together. Beat butter, sugar, molasses, and egg together until light and fluffy. Add sifted ingredients alternately with cold water. Beat until blended. Stir in raisins. Drop by rounded tablespoonfuls 3 inches apart on greased baking sheet. Bake 10 to 12 minutes at 350°. Size should be approximately 4 inches across.

BENNE SEED WAFERS

Benne or Sesame seeds are taken from the seed pods of an herb grown in any tropical climate. The plants were brought here by ship and grown in the southern part of this country.

½ cup sesame or benne seeds
1 cup unsifted all purpose flour
1/8 teaspoon salt
½ teaspoon soda
¾ cup butter or margarine, softened
1 cup light brown sugar, firmly packed
1 egg
1 teaspoon vanilla extract

Put benne seeds in a heavy skillet over medium heat, stirring constantly until seeds are golden brown. In a large bowl combine butter, brown sugar, egg, and vanilla, beating until smooth. Add flour that has been sifted with salt and soda, then toasted seeds, stirring until well blended. Freeze covered for two hours or refrigerate overnight.

Preheat oven to 375°. Drop dough from a slightly rounded teaspoon 2 inches apart onto ungreased cookie sheet. Bake 10 minutes until lightly browned around edge. Let stand one minute, then remove to cool. Makes 5 dozen.

STONEWARE JUG

COBBLESTONES

Chocolate from the West Indies would have been used sparingly in Mrs. Crane's kitchen, but with today's supply, school children visiting the Crane House can enjoy these little cakes baked in the beehive oven.

1 cup light brown sugar
½ cup butter or margarine
1 beaten egg
1½ cups sifted flour
½ teaspoon baking soda
½ teaspoon salt
1 teaspoon vanilla
½ cup cracked chocolate (chocolate drops)

Cream together the butter and sugar, add beaten egg and vanilla. Sift together flour, soda, salt, and stir into creamed mixture and beat well. Fold in chocolate. Drop from a heaping tablespoon onto a greased cookie sheet 3 inches apart. Bake at 375° for 12-15 minutes.

Another way: Substitute ½ cup white raisins for chocolate drops, and 1 teaspoon cinnamon.

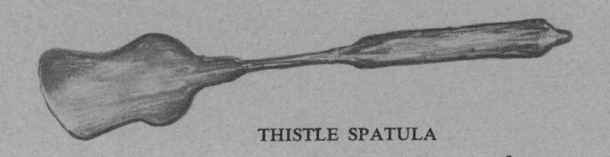

THISTLE SPATULA

APPLE BRANDY DROPS

1 cup light brown sugar
½ cup shortening
1 egg
1½ cups sifted flour
½ teaspoon soda
½ teaspoon salt
1 teaspoon nutmeg
1 cup chopped unpared apples

Cream sugar and shortening. Beat in egg, sift dry ingredients and add; beat well. Fold in apples. Form into balls, place on greased cookie sheet and bake at 375° for 12-15 minutes.

Straight from the oven pat each little cake with a linen cloth dipped into a generous amount of brandy.

HOSPITALITY THINS

Stamp these "little cakes" with a pineapple and serve them up for tea with friends.

2/3 cup soft butter
2 teaspoons grated lemon peel
2 teaspoons ground ginger
½ teaspoon baking soda
½ teaspoon salt
1 teaspoon vanilla extract
1 cup sugar
1 egg
3 tablespoons lemon juice
2 cups sifted flour

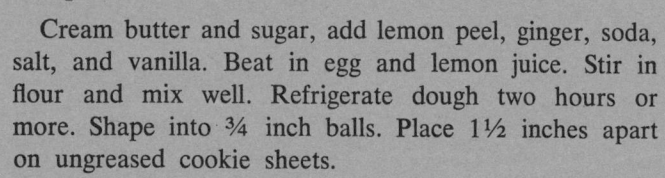

Cream butter and sugar, add lemon peel, ginger, soda, salt, and vanilla. Beat in egg and lemon juice. Stir in flour and mix well. Refrigerate dough two hours or more. Shape into ¾ inch balls. Place 1½ inches apart on ungreased cookie sheets.

Bake in preheated hot oven (400°) 6-8 minutes until set but not hard. Flatten with a pineapple butter stamp as soon as they come from the oven. 6 dozen.

Hospitality is a most excellent virtue; but care must be taken that the love of company, for its own sake, does not become a prevailing passion; for then the habit is no longer hospitality but dissipation.

PRINTED SPICE CRINKLES

You will need a butter print to stamp these little cakes hot from the oven. They were simple enough for the Crane children to make and fun to print. Today's children and grandchildren would like to try it too.

¾ cup soft butter or margarine
1 cup packed brown sugar
1 egg
¼ cup molasses
2¼ cups flour
2 teaspoons baking soda
2 teaspoons cinnamon
2 teaspoons ginger
¾ teaspoon cloves
¼ teaspoon salt

BUTTER MOLD

Mix butter, sugar, egg, and molasses in a bowl. In another bowl stir together flour, soda, spices, and salt. Mix dry ingredients into shortening mixture. Chill dough 2 hours or overnight.

Roll dough into balls the size of large walnuts. Dip tops in sugar. Place little cakes sugared side up 3 inches apart on baking sheet. Bake 375° 10-12 minutes until set but not hard.

Firmly press each little cake with a butter print as soon as it comes from the oven.

ROSEWATER-CURRANT CAKES

1 cup butter
1 cup sugar
1 tablespoon rosewater
3 eggs
2 cups flour
½ cup currants

Cream butter and sugar. Add eggs one at a time beating well. Stir in rosewater, then add flour and currants. Bake on cookie sheets in preheated 375° oven for 12-15 minutes or until edges brown.

Heart Cakes

Beat 1 pound butter to a cream with some rosewater 1 pound flour dryed 1 pound sifted sugar 12 eggs Beat all together Add a few currants washed and dryed Butter some small pans heart shaped pour in the mixture grate sugar over them They are soon baked in a Dutch oven.

On the Quality of Milk for Making Butter

The first requisite is to have a good cow. One that has high hips, short fore legs and a large udder is to be preferred. She should have a good pasture not far distant. Feed her once a day with the waste from the kitchen, adding to it about a pint of Indian Meal. Take care that nothing is given to her that will injure the milk such as turnips and parsnips.

MAIDS OF HONOR

Mrs. Crane would have served these elegant little almond tarts on very special occasions. Their preparation is time consuming, but so rewarding to the taste.

4 eggs
1 cup sugar
4 tablespoons flour
5 tablespoons melted butter
1 cup almond paste
Sherry
½ cup ground almonds
1 teaspoon nutmeg
Red currant jelly, especially homemade, or strawberry jam

Moisten almond paste with enough sherry to mix into medium paste consistency. Set aside to mellow for at least one hour. Butter smallest size muffin pans very well. Beat eggs for five minutes, then gradually add sugar mixed with flour. Mix in melted butter, ground almonds, and moistened almond paste.

Line muffin tins with rich pastry. Add ¼ teaspoon jelly or jam to center of pastry and cover with almond filling. Do not overfill. Bake at 350° for 25 minutes or until lightly browned on top, but not dark in color. Turn out of pans to cool.

BLACK WALNUT CAKES WITH MAPLE FROSTING

These little cakes will keep for weeks, if locked up.

½ teaspoon soda
½ teaspoon salt
1 teaspoon vanilla
1 cup black walnuts, chopped
1 cup light brown sugar
½ cup shortening
1 egg, beaten
1½ cups sifted flour

Cream sugar and shortening until very light. Add egg and vanilla. Sift together dry ingredients, stir into sugar mixture, then add walnut meats. Drop on greased cookie sheet, bake 375° for 12-15 minutes.

Maple Frosting

½ cup maple sugar
4 tablespoons butter
4 tablespoons thin cream
Confectioners' sugar

Over low heat cook maple sugar and butter until melted and bubbling. Remove from fire, add cream, beating until smooth. Add confectioners' sugar until it is thick enough to spread.

Note: If unable to obtain granulated maple sugar, substitute maple syrup, omit cream, add butter and heat until bubbling. Add ½ teaspoon maple flavoring. Mix with confectioners' sugar.

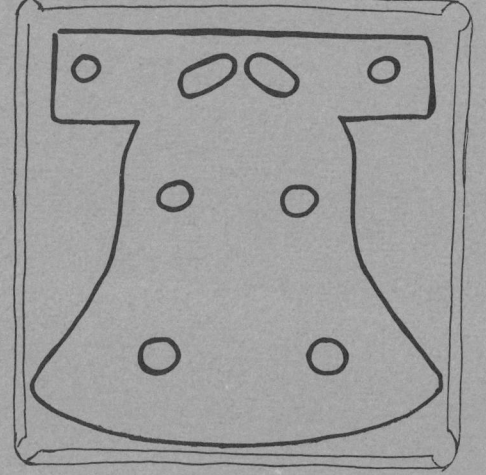

ROLLED HOLIDAY CAKES

1 cup sugar
½ pound butter
3 eggs well beaten
1 teaspoon mace
1/3 cup brandy
4 cups sifted flour

Cream butter and sugar until light and fluffy. Add the eggs and flavorings. Add flour and beat or knead until smooth. Roll into two rolls, wrap in paper, and chill for several hours.

Using one roll at a time, roll dough out on lightly floured board until 1/16 inch thick. Use the Crane House kitchen tin cutters—the horse, Liberty Bell, the hand, the gingerbread man or the star.

Place them carefully on unbuttered tins, sprinkle with chopped almonds and granulated sugar, and with a toothpick make a hole at the top for stringing. Candied angelica may be used for eyes and buttons. Bake at 375° until light golden, usually 8-10 minutes. Yield several dozen.

TIN CUTTERS

SUNDAY NIGHT WAFERS

A wafer iron, richly ornamented, initialed, and dated was a traditional gift to a bride. Fanny Pierson Crane enjoyed the pleasant task of making wafers on Sunday night while her family watched and waited.

4 beaten eggs
1 cup sugar
¼ pound melted butter
1¼ cups graham or white flour
Pinch salt
½ teaspoon mace

Take your wafer iron and warm it in the coals. Mix all things together. Put one tablespoon batter in center of heated iron. Count to 6. Peel wafer off with two tined fork. Reheat wafer iron and repeat. Take care iron is not too hot.

If you wish, roll hot wafer immediately into a cone, then fill with fresh berries and heavy cream whipped up.

WAFER IRON

MISS MARY'S MERINGUES
(Kisses for Dessert Pyramids)

3 egg whites
1 teaspoon vanilla
¼ teaspoon cream of tartar
Dash salt
1 cup sugar
Red and green food color

In a creamware mixing bowl, combine egg whites, vanilla, cream of tartar, and salt; beat to soft peaks. Very gradually add sugar, beating until very stiff peaks form. Meringue should be glossy. Add cochineal (red food color) to some, and spinach juice (green food color) to the rest. Drop from tablespoon onto ungreased baking sheet about 1½ inches apart, and bake in a slack oven (275°) for 30 minutes or more. Immediately remove from tin and cool.

Uncommon Cakes and Pies

GLAZED ORANGE CAKE

Oranges found their way to Cranetown from Louisiana or the West Indies, into Israel Crane's General Store, and thus into the cooking kitchen of Fanny Crane.

Chopped rind of 1 orange
1 cup golden raisins
½ cup butter
1 cup sugar
2 beaten eggs
1 teaspoon vanilla
2 cups flour
1 teaspoon baking soda
½ teaspoon salt
1 cup buttermilk

FIREDOGS

Take a Seville orange rind, chopped very fine, and add the golden raisins. Blend butter with sugar, add eggs, vanilla, and chopped mixture. Sift flour with soda and salt. Add to creamed mixture alternately with buttermilk. Turn into well-greased 9 x 9 x 2 pan or 2 well greased loaf pans. Bake in 350° oven for 30-40 minutes. Can be doubled with success.

Glaze

1 cup sugar
Orange juice to moisten
Brandy to flavor

Spread glaze on warm cake, and sizzle with a red hot salamander or peel. If utensils are not available, place briefly under high broiler until the glaze sizzles. Slice into small squares and serve warm with herbed tea sprigged with orange mint. The Crane House ladies' favorite cake.

The salamander was the animal in mythology who could go through fire unharmed . . . thus the 18th century name given to the glazing tool.

IRON PEEL

Supper Served in the Warming Kitchen

Visitors often enjoyed the simple elegance of Fanny Pierson Crane's hospitality at supper parties.

Mock Clary

Cider and Brown-Sugared Ham   Baked Elizabethtown Crab
Maced Green Beans   Carrot Pudding

Madeira Molded Jelly

Hot Pumpkin Bread   Molded Butter Prints   Crab Apple and Rosemary Jelly
Tomato-Ginger Preserves   Rose Geranium Jelly

Sampling of Sweets

Tansy Pie   Coriander Ginger Cake   Rosewater-Currant Cakes
Glazed Orange Cake   Cobblestones
Abigail's Soft Molasses Cakes
Madeira   Nut Meats   Port

An Evening Collation

To entertain a goodly number of people the dining room table was covered with meats, pastries, cakes, confections, fools, flummeries, nuts and dainties of all kinds, first to be admired and then to be sampled. To refresh the spirit, an exceeding good punch was always served.

Ham from the Smokehouse   Native Stuffed and Roasted Turkey
Cheddar Biscuits   Mushroom Savouries
Flowers and Fruit in White Wine Jelly

Dessert Pyramids

Kisses
Ginger Cakes
Savoy Biscuits
Macaroons

Glazed Orange Cake   Maids of Honor   Printed Spice Crinkles
Black Walnut Patties   Benne Seed Wafers   Carrot Tea Cake
Chocolate Truffles   Whiskey Nut Balls   Candied Peel   Almonds
Grandmother Pierson's Pound Cake
Tipsy Squire

New Jersey Stone Fence Punch   Rose Geranium Spiced Tea Punch

Lighting the Beehive Oven was a tedious chore undertaken only once a week except at holiday time. For everyday baking, Fanny Crane used her Dutch Oven, hanging from the crane. Both receipts do well this way. The aroma of coriander makes the first unique, the second the flavor of ginger and orange.

CORIANDER GINGER CAKE

2 beaten eggs
1 cup molasses
½ cup sugar
½ cup butter
1 tablespoon ginger root, grated
1 teaspoon cloves
1 teaspoon cinnamon
1 teaspoon salt
1 heaping tablespoon ground coriander
2½ cups flour
2 teaspoons baking soda
1 cup hot water
½ cup white raisins
½ cup nuts

Mix molasses, sugar, butter. Add beaten eggs, spices, and salt. Sift flour three times with soda. To butter mixture add dry ingredients alternately with hot water. Stir in raisins and nuts. Bake in 325° about 40 minutes.

DUTCH OVEN GINGERBREAD

1 egg, well beaten
½ cup sugar
½ cup dark molasses
¼ cup butter
½ cup hot water
2 cups cake flour, sifted
¼ teaspoon salt
1 teaspoon ginger
1 teaspoon cinnamon
1 teaspoon soda
1 tablespoon grated orange rind

Combine and beat well the egg, sugar and molasses. Mix butter into hot water and stir until melted. Add butter mixture to sugar, egg, and molasses.

Sift the dry ingredients together, add to other mixture in three parts, beating after each addition only until well blended. Pour into lightly greased mold, bake at 350° for about 50 minutes.

DUTCH OVEN

TANSY PIE

6 eggs, separated
1 pint heavy cream
½ cup granulated sugar
½ cup white wine or sherry
¼ pound Naples biscuits (lady fingers), broken up
½ tablespoon nutmeg
Fresh or dried tansy — 3 sprigs (few drops of green food coloring optional)
1 pastry lined 10 inch pie plate

Place egg yolks in a saucepan and beat slightly. Stir in cream, sugar, sherry, then add biscuits and nutmeg. Cook, stirring until the mixture thickens. Add green coloring if desired, but give preference to tansy pressed in a stone mortar until it becomes pulpy and juices are evident.

Beat egg whites until they form stiff peaks, and fold into the hot cream mixture. Pour into the pastry-lined pie plate. Bake at 450° for 10 minutes, then reduce to 350° and bake for 30 minutes longer.

The pie will be puffy and golden but may sink somewhat as it cools. Garnish with rounded mounds of whipped cream sprigged with fresh tansy and dusted with nutmeg. Take to the table on a footed cake stand.

Beloved tansy, first herb to greet the springtime, was used for spring tonics needed after long hard winters . . . here it is used not only for flavoring but also as the green coloring agent for 18th century cooking.

STONE MORTAR

Original

Beat seven eggs, yolks and whites separately; add a pint of cream, near the same spinach juice, and a little tansey juice gained by pounding in a stonemortar; a quarter of a pound of Naples biscuit, sugar to taste, a glass of white wine, and some nutmeg. Set all in a saucepan, just to thicken, over the fire; then put into a dish, line with paste to turn out and bake it.

GRANDMOTHER PIERSON'S DATED POUND CAKE

½ pint heavy cream
2 eggs
1 cup sugar
1½ cups sifted flour
1 teaspoon vanilla

Beat cream in large bowl until stiff. In another bowl beat eggs until frothy. Add eggs to cream, beating at medium speed, then mix in rest of ingredients. Bake in two buttered, floured 8 inch round cake pans at 350° for 20-25 minutes or until tests done.

Grandmother Pierson's pound cake is an adaption of an 18th century receipt used for family festivities or "entertainments," most especially wedding receptions or teas.

Date Topping

1 pound dates, pitted and halved
Honey
Few drops lemon juice
Whole blanched almonds

Place dates, honey, and lemon juice in pan and gently warm on low heat. The dates should retain their shape. Allow to cool slightly.

Arrange date halves and almonds on top of each cake in an attractive circular pattern, alternating dates and nuts. Pour small amount of honey over top of each cake and allow to stand for a few minutes. Repeat once more after honey has been absorbed by cake.

This receipt makes two cakes.

WHISKEY APPLE PIE

*"and there they hung them for the flies
'til mother turned them into pies."*

12 ounces dried apples
1 cup whiskey, or applejack (which is preferred)
1 cup cider
1 cup brown sugar*
1 teaspoon cinnamon
1 teaspoon ginger
Generous grating of nutmeg
9 inch uncooked pie crust

Soak dried apples in 1 cup whiskey or applejack and 1 cup cider for several hours or overnight. If apples are still quite dry add enough cider to barely cover, cook 10 minutes over medium heat to soften. Add brown sugar, cinnamon, ginger, and nutmeg to apples and juice. Place mixture in pastry shell, dot with butter. Bake in pre-heated 400° oven for 20-25 minutes. Watch carefully and lace with extra cider if necessary. This pie has no top crust and will be flat in appearance.

General Maxim for Health
Rise early. Eat simple food. Take plenty of exercise. Never fear a little fatigue.

CARROT TEA CAKE

Carrots from the root cellar make this uncommon cake a mid-winter treat. For her sewing circle Fanny Crane served it on her best china in the front parlor.

¾ cup plus 2 tablespoons corn oil
2 cups sugar
4 beaten eggs
2 cups finely grated raw carrots
2 cups flour
1 teaspoon salt
2 teaspoons baking soda
3 teaspoons cinnamon
1 teaspoon nutmeg

Mix oil, sugar, eggs, and carrots together. Add flour, salt, baking soda, cinnamon, and nutmeg. Bake in #2 spring form pan for 1 hour at 350°.

A bundt pan may be used instead if greased well. Serve with a dusting of sugar and slice very thin.

Jellies & Preserves

MADEIRA WINE JELLY GARNISHED WITH FROSTED FRUIT

Wine Jelly

4 envelopes plain gelatin
½ cup cold water
2 cups grape juice
¾ - 1 cup sugar
Pinch salt
1 pint Madeira wine
6 tablespoons strained fresh lemon juice

Frosted Fruit

Strawberries
Green grapes
Purple grapes
Strawberry or nasturtium leaves if in season

Dissolve gelatin in cold water. Add this to the grape juice that has been brought to a boil. Stir in Madeira, lemon juice, and a pinch of salt. Add sugar to taste. Pour into your mold. An old tin one is nicest. Chill until firm.

Unmold and garnish with Frosted Fruit. To frost, dip fruit first in slightly beaten egg whites and then roll in granulated sugar. Dry on a rack overnight at room temperature.

Arrange fruit and leaves in a pretty fashion around Wine Jelly, and serve as a complement to meat or as a dessert with brandied custard sauce.

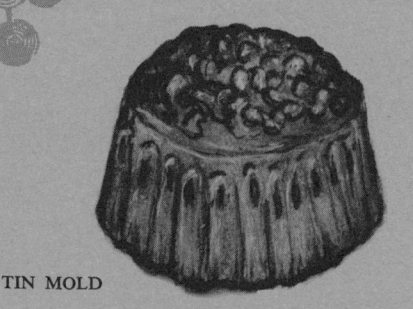

TIN MOLD

ROSE GERANIUM JELLY

Wash apples, not too ripe, cut in pieces without paring or coring. Barely cover with water (2 cups water to 4 cups of fruit) and boil until very soft. Pour all into a jelly bag or several layers of cheesecloth; hang it over a container and allow to drip overnight. Do not squeeze or apple juice will be cloudy.

To 2 cups juice add 2 cups sugar and the juice of ½ lemon. Boil until syrup will jell. Skim. Place two rose geranium leaves in the bottom of each warm jelly glass. Pour in hot jelly and cover with paraffin.

Especially pleasing with Sally Lunn and other tea breads.

CRABAPPLE ROSEMARY JELLY

"Rosemary for remembrance"

5 cups crabapples (enough to yield 1 quart)
2 cups water
1½ to 2 cups sugar
Fresh rosemary

Gather fresh crabapples. Wash and drain. Cut out the ends. Chop in half and measure (there should be 1 quart). Combine apples with water, cover, simmer until fruit is soft. Drain through 4 layers of cheesecloth.

Measure juice into a large saucepan. For each cup juice add ¾-1 cup sugar and boil rapidly to the jellying point (220° candy thermometer). As the jelly cooks, swirl fresh rosemary branches in the liquid. Remove jelly from heat and skim off foam.

Fill sterilized jars with jelly leaving ½ inch head space. Add one clean sprig of rosemary to each jelly glass. Seal with paraffin. Yield: 2 to 4 half pints of jelly.

TOMATO-GINGER PRESERVES

1 pound red tomatoes
1 pound sugar
2 thinly sliced seeded lemons
2 ounces crystalized ginger, chopped

Scald, skin, and slice tomatoes. Cover them with equal amount of sugar and permit them to stand for 12 hours. Drain the juice, and boil it until the syrup falls from a spoon in heavy drops. Add the tomatoes, sliced lemons, and ginger. Cook the preserves until they are thick and clear. Pack in hot jars and seal.

Serve with Sally Lunn for tea, as a meat complement, or spread generously on home-baked white bread.

CRANBERRY CONSERVE

4 cups (1 pound) fresh cranberries
1 large orange
1 cup golden raisins
¼ cup honey
¾ cup sugar
1½ teaspoons ginger
½ cup chopped walnuts

Quarter orange and remove seeds. Put with cranberries through a food chopper. Mix with raisins, nuts, honey, sugar, and ginger. So that flavors may blend chill in refrigerator several hours. Makes 4 cups.

FLOWERS AND FRUIT IN WHITE WINE JELLY

3 envelopes unflavored gelatin
1 cup water
1 cup sugar
1 bottle white wine (4/5 quart)
4 tablespoons fresh lemon juice, strained
3 well washed damask, rugosa, or moss roses (or deep red modern roses in full bloom)
Seedless grapes
Rose leaves

Heat gelatin and water in medium saucepan until dissolved. Add sugar and white wine. Heat until sugar is melted and mixture steams. Stir in strained lemon juice. Pour ¼ inch gelatin mixture into an 8 inch ring mold.

Set in freezer for 10 minutes or until just softly firm. Press in roses, grapes and a few rose leaves in a pleasing pattern. Pour a small amount of mixture on top but not so much or flowers will float.

Place in freezer for 10 minutes. Then very slowly pour remaining mixture into mold. Return to freezer 10 minutes more. Remove to refrigerator.

When firm, unmold on silver tray. Serve plain with fish or fowl. Other flowers, herbs, and fruits may be substituted for the roses: Gilly flowers (dianthus) and strawberries; pot marigold, nasturtiums, and lemon balm.

Wine Jelly
Take 4 calves feet, and wash them well without taking off the hoofs (or instead of that 1 oz. isinglass, or 1 oz. of deer horns). These feet must be well boiled the day before they are wanted. After taking off the grease put the jelly in a casserole.

Confections

CANDIED PEEL

November and December brought a flurry of excitement to the Israel Crane General Store with the unloading of crates of oranges and grapefruits, bags of coconuts, boxes of figs, and sometimes, a few pineapples. These were rarely seen at any other season. Today, confections utilizing some of these luxuries are made in the Crane House kitchen at Christmas-time.

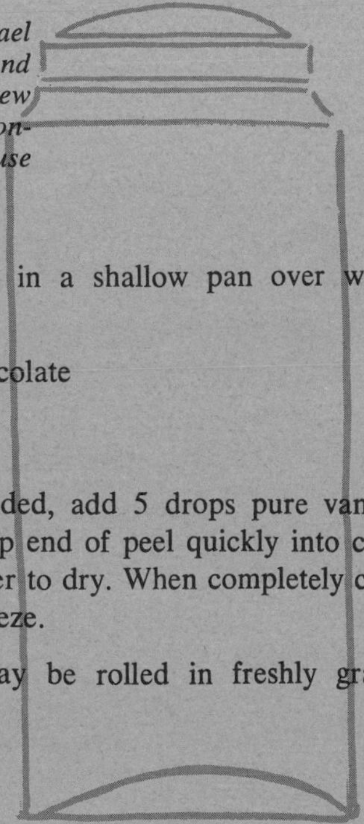

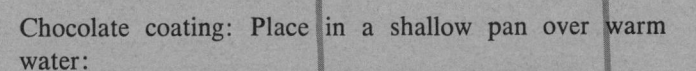

Cut rind of 4 oranges and 3 grapefruits into quarters. Cover with cold water. Bring slowly to the boiling point. Remove pan from fire. Drain well. Repeat this process, boiling the peel in a total of 5 waters. Drain well each time. With scissors, cut into strips or leaf design.

For 1 grapefruit or 2 oranges, make a syrup allowing ¼ cup water and ½ cup sugar. Add the peel, and boil it until all the syrup is absorbed. Cool briefly. Roll it in granulated sugar and spread to dry on waxed paper. When thoroughly dry, the peel may be dipped at one end in chocolate coating:

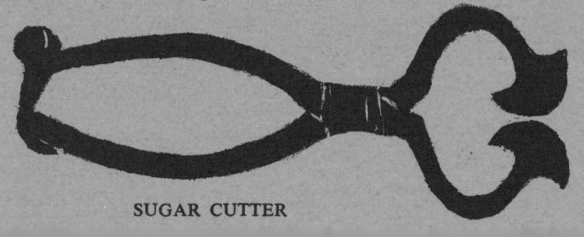

Chocolate coating: Place in a shallow pan over warm water:

4 ounces semi-sweet chocolate
2 tablespoons butter
1 inch square paraffin

When melted and blended, add 5 drops pure vanilla. Remove from heat and dip end of peel quickly into coating. Return to waxed paper to dry. When completely cool, store in airtight tins or freeze.

Another way: Peel may be rolled in freshly grated coconut, then sugared.

SUGAR CUTTER

WHISKEY NUT BALLS

50 pecan halves
100 proof bourbon, enough to cover nutmeats
1 stick butter, softened
2 boxes confectioners' sugar
5 squares semi-sweet chocolate
Paraffin — 1 inch square
2 tablespoons butter

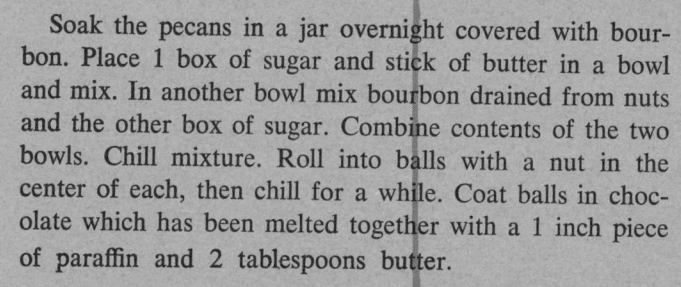

Soak the pecans in a jar overnight covered with bourbon. Place 1 box of sugar and stick of butter in a bowl and mix. In another bowl mix bourbon drained from nuts and the other box of sugar. Combine contents of the two bowls. Chill mixture. Roll into balls with a nut in the center of each, then chill for a while. Coat balls in chocolate which has been melted together with a 1 inch piece of paraffin and 2 tablespoons butter.

These special confections should be stored in a tin in a cool place. They will disappear if you turn your head.

BLOWN GLASS JARS

CHOCOLATE TRUFFLES

When Thomas Jefferson moved into the White House in 1801, he brought with him a fondness for French cookery and customs, acquired when he was American Minister to France. His influence was felt throughout the states, and none less in the Crane household, where the French Chocolate Truffles found their place on the Collation table.

6 squares or 6 ounces semi-sweet chocolate
¼ cup sifted confectioners' sugar
3 tablespoons butter
3 slightly beaten egg yolks
1 tablespoon brandy
Grated chocolate — 2 squares semi-sweet
½ teaspoon cinnamon

In top of double boiler over hot but not boiling water, melt squares of chocolate with sugar and butter. Remove from heat. Stir a small amount of hot mixture into slightly beaten egg yolks; return to hot mixture, stirring well. Blend in brandy. Chill, without stirring, for 1 to 2 hours. Shape in 1 inch balls. Finely grate 2 squares (2 ounces) semi-sweet chocolate. Add cinnamon. Roll balls in grated mixture. Store in refrigerator.

TIPSY SQUIRE

Savoy Biscuit or Sponge Cake

6 extra large eggs, separated and at room temperature
2/3 cup sugar
3 tablespoons lemon juice
2/3 cup sifted flour
½ teaspoon salt
Grated rind of one lemon

Beat egg yolks until very light, slowly beat in sugar, then lemon juice and lemon rind. Beat egg whites until stiff, then lightly fold into yolk mixture. Sift flour and salt together over egg combination and fold lightly.

Bake in buttered, floured long loaf pan at 300° for 7 minutes. Turn up oven to 325° for another 18 minutes. Do not overbake. Best if made day before using.

Custard Filling

1 envelope unflavored gelatin
4 tablespoons cold water
8 egg yolks
1 cup sugar
2 cups milk, scalded
1 teaspoon vanilla
1 tablespoon almond extract
2 cups heavy cream
Toasted half almonds

Soak gelatin in cold water. Beat egg yolks until light in color, then gradually add sugar, beating all the while. Add a little of yolk mixture to scalded milk, then add the milk to the yolks stirring constantly. Add vanilla and almond extracts. Rest a pottery bowl on a large pan of boiling water, so that bottom of bowl is approximately 2 inches above water. Cook, stirring constantly until smooth, slightly thickened, and coats a wooden spoon. Mixture will have consistency of thin to medium cream sauce and will thicken as it cools.

Remove from heat, add softened gelatin, stirring until gelatin is dissolved. Cool, stirring occasionally to prevent a thickened layer from forming on the top. Just before assembling Tipsy Squire, fold in heavy cream, whipped.

Rum
2 cups heavy cream, whipped
Candied violets, roses
Nutmeg

To assemble: Cut Savoy Biscuit into dainty fingers ¼ inch thick. Arrange decoratively around sides and bottom of best glass compote. Sprinkle generously with rum and let soak in for at least one hour. Spoon custard into center and spike surface with toasted almonds so entire area is covered with nuts about 1 inch apart. Pile whipped cream in tall peaks about 1 inch apart around the outside rim of the compote. Mound cream in high peaks in center of compote in an even, symetrical manner.

Dust with freshly grated nutmeg. Decorate each peak of cream with a candied violet or rose. Receipt makes two compotes of Tipsy Squire.

Note: It is important to the authenticity of this receipt to make the peaks of cream quite high.

In Fanny Crane's day, this elegant dessert was made with stale cake, restored to full flavour with liberal sprinklings of rum. It was served to the squire or parson and honored guests, who became a little "tipsy" after abundant helpings of this favorite sweet.

40

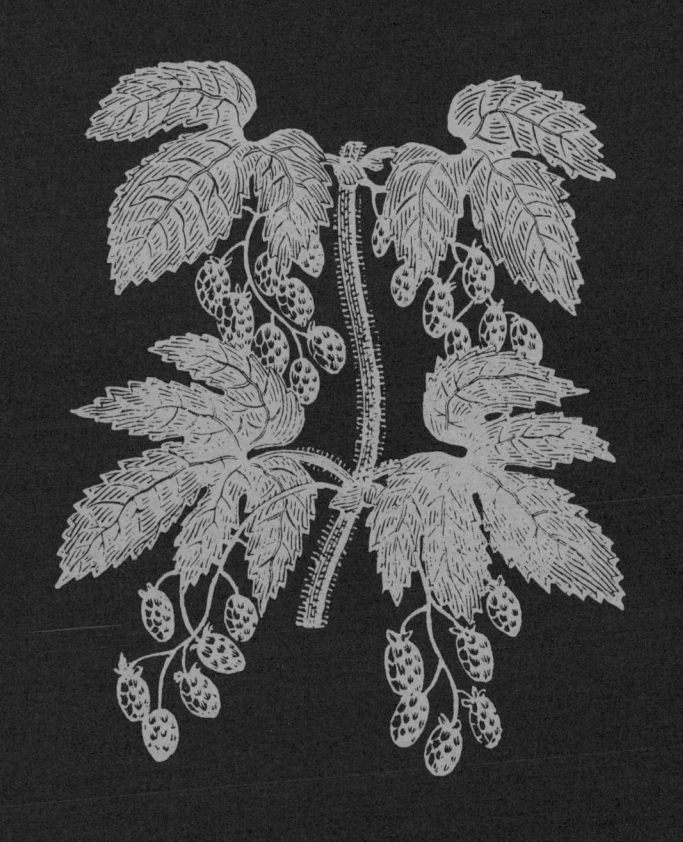

CROCK-PRESERVED FRUITS

The hearty appetites of eighteenth century Englishmen and their relatives in the middle colonies encouraged housewives to put down fruits in fine brandy or rum. The custom spread with the settlement of the country until preserved fruits became familiar on butt'ry shelves everywhere.

Take only well-ripened fragrant fruits, each as in season. First thoroughly wash strawberries and soak them in rum . . . they will probably float for one day before they sink. Then add cherries, gooseberries, red currants, raspberries, mirabelle plums, apricots, peaches, and if desired, sliced pears. For an extra touch of flavour, use fresh pineapple. DO NOT use apples, black currants, or blackberries. Use the same weight of sugar as of fruit, and to avoid any fermentation, half the liquid should be rum. Care should be taken to see that the fruits are always covered with liquid and that the jar is airtight.

When a new layer of fruit in season is added, add more rum, and the weight of the fruit in sugar. It takes 6 weeks for one layer to mature. Do not stir.

After adding last layer of fruit, let rest for six weeks. Stir well before you serve fruits. This is lovely with a sugared ham, but is cherished as a holiday dessert with freshly churned vanilla ice cream.

GREENGAGE PLUM ICE CREAM

Gathering greengage plums from one's garden for this delicious and elegant ice cream would have been a delightful chore. Happily, one can buy the preserves today, as a scarcity of these fruits now exists.

1 pint greengage plum preserves
Juice of 2 lemons
2 cups sugar
1½ quarts milk
1 quart cream
Pinch salt

Mix all together. Freeze in a crank or electric freezer. Fill scooped out oranges or lemon halves and garnish with a candied flower. These can be done in advance and frozen until serving time.

Place on a galax leaf (can be purchased from a florist).

IRON LADLE

ROSE GERANIUM CREAM FOR BERRIES

1 cup heavy cream
¼ cup sugar
2 rose geranium leaves
8 ounces cream cheese

Combine heavy cream, sugar, and rose geranium leaves in top of double boiler. With wooden spoon bruise rose geranium leaves in the cream so the flavor is absorbed by the liquid. Heat slowly over hot water but do not let boil. Cool, then remove leaves. Add cream slowly to cream cheese until well mixed.

Chill cream until ready to serve with blackberries, blueberries, huckleberries, or raspberries. A treat for a summer day. Present each serving in a glass dish with a spoonful of cream on top, and a rose geranium leaf crowning the whole.

RASPBERRY OR GOOSEBERRY FOOL

1 quart ripe gooseberries or raspberries
¼ cup water
1 cup sugar
1½ teaspoons grated lemon rind
1½ cups heavy cream

Combine berries with water in a saucepan. Cook over low heat until fruit is extremely tender. Remove from heat and puree. Stir in sugar and lemon rind. Set aside to cool. Whip cream and stir into puree.

Spoon into a pretty bowl and chill. Garnish with fresh berries. Serve with small macaroons.

Savouries

MUSHROOM SAVOURIES

¾ cup butter
3 medium onions, chopped
2 pounds fresh mushrooms, finely chopped
4 tablespoons fresh thyme or 2 tablespoons dry
¾ cup white wine or sherry
½ cup parsley, chopped
2 teaspoons salt
Pastry dough

Filling: Sauté onions in butter until golden. Add mushrooms, thyme, salt, and parsley. Simmer for five minutes. add sherry. Simmer until liquid is almost absorbed. Cool.

Roll pastry dough very thin. Cut into 2½ inch circles. Place filling on one half of circle. Fold over and crimp with five fingers. Moisten edges. Bake on ungreased tin in moderate oven until golden brown. Yield approximately 200 savouries.

Observation
And as it is difficult to ascertain with precision the small articles of spicery; every one may relish as they like, and suit their taste.

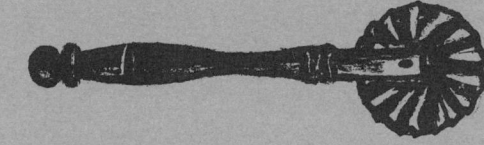

PASTRY JIG

BRASS GRATER

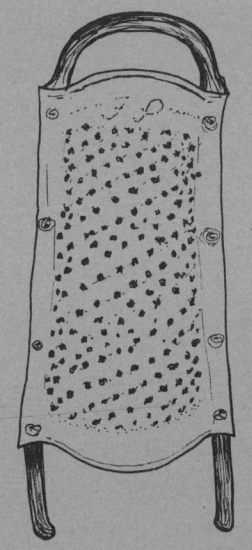

CHEDDAR BISCUITS

½ cup butter
½ pound sharp unprocessed cheddar, grated
1½ cups all purpose flour
½ teaspoon salt
¼ teaspoon cayenne pepper
Blanched almonds or pecans

Cream the butter and cheese and mix in flour, salt and pepper. (Chill and roll into rolls the diameter of a half dollar.) Chill overnight.

Slice about 1/3 to 1/2 inch thick. Press half an almond or pecan in the center of each biscuit. Use an ungreased cookie sheet sprinkled lightly with salt. Bake 7 or 8 minutes at 350°. Makes 6 dozen. These keep beautifully in a closed tin.

ALMONDS FOR A COLLATION

After the main courses were served, the second cloth was removed and fruit and nuts were set on the bare table along with Madeira and Port. Usually nuts were presented in the shell, but this is another way.

Take your shelled almonds and blanche them. Remove skins. Saute in butter in a fry pan or spider until nicely brown. Shake in a paper bag to which salt has been added. This removes excess oils and coats nuts well. Allow to cool; then tin.

JERSEY SKILLET APPLES

6 large apples, Red Delicious or Cortland
1 cup sugar
1 cup water
1 cup rose geranium flavored applejack

Core and peel top third of each apple. Combine the peelings with sugar, water, rose geranium flavored applejack in a large iron skillet. Boil 10 minutes, strain and return to skillet.

Place a lightly buttered rose geranium leaf in each apple and arrange in pan with juices. Cook the apples over moderate heat, turning them frequently until just tender, but hold their shape. Ladle pan juices over apples as they cook.

Rose Geranium Applejack

To one pint applejack add 4 or 5 mature rose geranium leaves, letting combination steep for 3 weeks. If the aroma and strength are still not suitable remove the old leaves and add new ones, steeping another week.

This infusion will be most enjoyable added to sliced fruit, compotes, custards, meringue toppings, meat marinades and basting sauces.

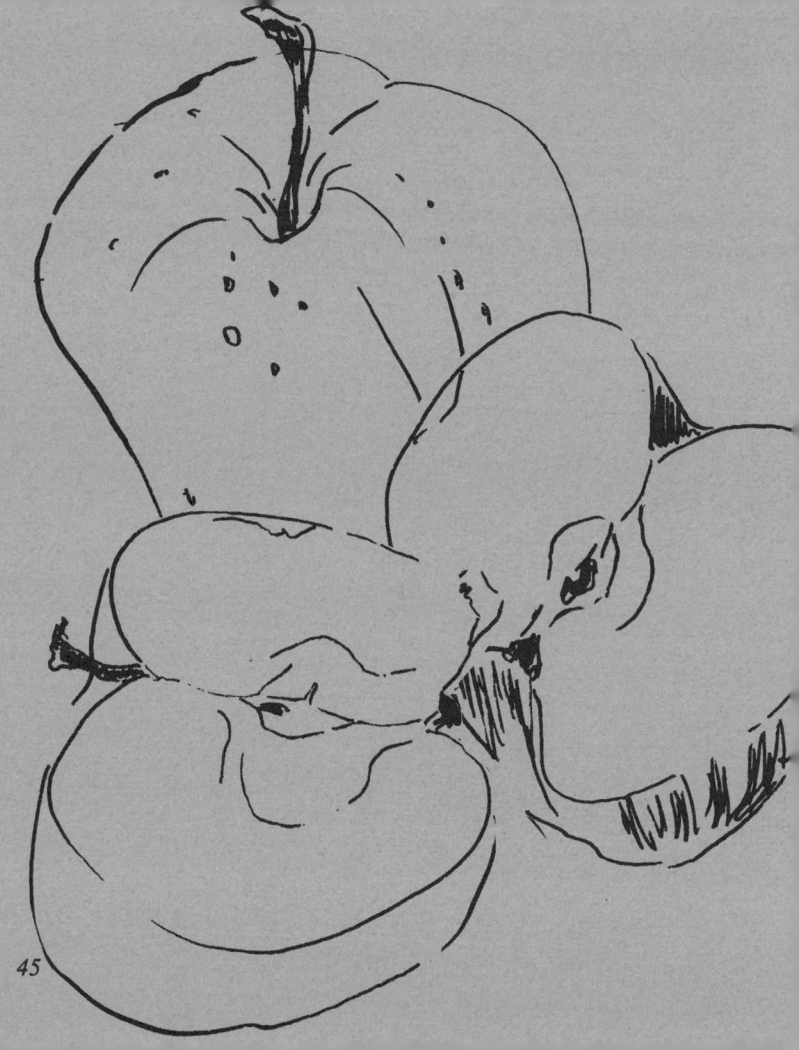

Drams

CRANETOWN MULLED CYDER

Apple cyder, the common drink in town, was made by Israel Crane in his Cider Mill, which stood to the east of his General Store. For this spicy concoction, use only fresh sweet cider and permit no substitute.

1 gallon cider
1 tablespoon whole allspice
1 tablespoon whole cloves
12 sticks cinnamon
2 teaspoons whole nutmeg, grated
1 cup orange juice
Juice of 3 lemons
Sugar to taste

Tie allspice, cloves and cinnamon in a cheesecloth bag. Bring cider, juices, and spices to boiling point; then heat 15 minutes to develop flavor. Serve piping hot. Small firmly baked apples spiked with cloves look nice in the punch bowl. Sprig each punch cup with apple mint.

NOGGIN

LOWESTOFT BOWL

NEW JERSEY STONE FENCE PUNCH

Potent Applejack or "Jersey Lightning" was made in Cranetown stills. This punch especially pleases the gentlemen. Two cups and a man can leap a stone fence.

1 quart applejack
1 quart fresh sweet cider
1 quart cold sparkling water

Pour all at once over ice ring into punch bowl and stir until well mingled. Garnish with lemon and orange slices studded with cloves. Serve in punch cups. This makes 30 servings. Allow 3 servings a person.

ROSE GERANIUM SPICED TEA PUNCH

A pungent aroma filled the room and made our hearts merry . . .

6 cups sugar
3 cups water
20 cinnamon sticks
6 tablespoons cloves
6 teaspoons nutmeg
Grated rind of 1 lemon
Grated rind of 1 orange
1 cup orange juice
6 tablespoons lemon juice
16 teaspoons tea (16 tea bags)
2 cups rose geranium leaves dried

In a saucepan blend sugar, water, orange, and lemon juice, orange and lemon rind grated, and a cheesecloth bag containing the cinnamon sticks, whole cloves, and nutmeg. Bring to a boil, stirring to dissolve sugar, and simmer gently for 10 minutes. This can be done well ahead of serving time.

About 30 minutes before serving time, pour 4 quarts boiling water over tea bags or tea, and steep for approximately 5 minutes. Remove the tea, warm the prepared spiced juice mixture, remove the spice bag, then combine with tea. Simmer gently, then crush the dried rose geranium leaves. Continue to simmer until the infusion suits your taste. Correct seasonings. Remove from heat and strain.

Because the sugar is added beforehand the tea becomes a punch, and can therefore be ladled piping hot from your loveliest Lowestoft punch bowl.

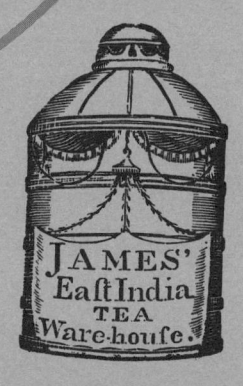

To Make a Fine Syllabub from the Cow

Sweeten a pint of Rhenish, half a pint of Sack, and one lemon with fine sugar. Grate nutmeg into it. Then milk your cow into your liquor. When you have thus added what quantity of milk you think proper, pour half a pint or more of the sweetest cream you can get over it. Then beat it all together to a froth.

Flip

Put a spoonful of brown sugar into 6 gills of malt beer, which is warmed by putting a hot iron or a loggerhead into it; afterwards, half a pint of rum is added and the mixture well stirred. Then a little nutmeg is grated on top which makes the flip fit for use. It is nourishing and strengthening, but in some constitutions, it excites a pain in the head.

MOCK CLARY

To 1 gallon claret, add enough honey to sweeten considerably. Add several pieces of cinnamon bark or sticks, some whole cloves, and freshly ground allspice. Place in a large pot hanging over fire or resting on hearth comfortably close to the fire to warm well, but not boil or burn.

Before it gets too warm, be sure to taste for perfect blending of spices and honey, as it may want more honey. Serve in warmed cups and all who drink will enjoy themselves.

THE EMPIRE MODE
1800

EMPIRE ROOM PUNCH

1 bottle rum
1 bottle brandy
1 bottle port wine
1 bottle white wine (or strong tea)
Juice of 10 lemons
½ pint curacao
3 cups white sugar

Take rind of squeezed lemons and add to stock. Stir well. Let stand for a couple of hours. Strain and bottle stock in ordinary wine bottles. When punch is needed, take 8 bottles of soda to 4 bottles of stock with plenty of ice. Stir well and serve. Will serve 25 to 30 people. Serve in a Limoge punch bowl and float roses on the top.

RUM-TEA PUNCH

1 can frozen lemonade concentrate, undiluted
½ cup liquid instant tea
4 cups cold water
½ cup superfine sugar
¾ cup amber rum
¼ cup brandy
1 lemon thinly sliced

In a large bowl, combine lemonade, tea, sugar and cold water. Stir until well blended. Add rum, brandy, and lemon slices. You may wish to add either more lemonade or more rum according to your taste. Pour over an ice ring in punch bowl. Garnish with mint. Makes 12 servings in 4 ounce punch cups.

To make a pretty ice ring, freeze lemon and orange slices with mint sprigs in a ring mold.

Potpourri and Sweet-Scents

It was the duty of Fanny Crane, a proper housewife, to make potpourri, pomanders, and sweet-scented bags. The aroma of fresh flowers and herbs mingled with spices not only cleansed the air, but filled the rooms with sweet and pungent fragrance.

Pot-pourri from the Pleasure Garden

10 cups rose petals, picked in the morning at the peak of their fragrance. Dry thoroughly in any room indoors.
½ ounce each ground cloves, cinnamon and allspice
3 ounces orris root

Mix well in a crockery bowl. Cover lightly and allow to mellow for several weeks stirring now and then with a wooden spoon. With this mixture you can add jasmine, rosebuds, geranium leaves, rosemary, marjoram or any other fragrant flower. Sniff constantly, always keeping the rose scent predominant. To enhance the fragance, add drops of essential oil of roses.

Fragrant Lemon Potpourri

Gather fragrant herbs, hang them to dry, mix the dried leaves as it pleases your senses.

1 cupful of lemon verbena
1 cupful of lemon balm
A handful of scented geraniums, bee balm, sweet woodruff, or orange mint
Rind of a lemon, dried and grated
1 ounce orris root

To strengthen the scent, add a few drops of lemon verbena oil. Fill small linen or silk bags and tie up with dainty ribbons. These will freshen your drawers and closets.

Orris root and essential oils can be procured from a trustworthy apothecary.

Sage for long life.

Fanny Pierson Crane, the daughter of a doctor, knew much about the curing properties of medicinal herbs. She had a sizeable herb garden and was well known in the village for her herbal teas and infusions which were used to tend the sick.

She was asked most often for her Feverfew tea, which reportedly reduced fever.

FEVERFEW. C. v. d. P. (*Compositæ.*)

HARVARD PRINTING CO.